daisy chain s

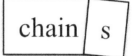

a debut collection of poems and prose by

Kay Riches

Cover by Kay Riches (acrylic on paper, 2021)
ISBN: 979-8-5964-4017-1

about

daisy chains follows a young writer through the transition of teenager to young adulthood on the path of recovery. This book travels through themes of love, mental health, self-awareness and self-acceptance, highlighting growing pains not just personal, but within our society.

The writer uses raw emotion and a whole load of uncomfortable questions (as well as fridge magnets) to heal and come to terms with the inevitability of growth. It may make you feel uneasy at times, empowered at others. Hopefully it will feel like a friend.

Trigger warnings: brief mentions of self-harm, suicidal thoughts, sexual abuse and eating disorders.

Than_

"If a writer falls in love with you, you can never die."
– Mik Everett

content s

there once was a girl
with eyes like wildflowers.
her skin glowed
because of all the stardust.

she sat in a little yellow boat
on a softly spoken river,
her hair was being played with
by the wind.

the river whispered
"you are pure gold"
but she drank all the yellow paint
and ate sunflowers anyway.

is it part of the human condition to crave to be more than
    you are?
how do you deal with that kind of pain?
the ache of being small,
the frustration
perhaps embedded from when you were little
and would cry because you weren't tall enough to reach
    the door handle.
I'm not sure that feeling ever goes away.
except the door handle is
a light switch,
a pay check,
a dream,
a person.
you forget about the door handle
but once upon a time it was the only thing you wanted.
now you reach for the next thing.
one day you'll forget that too.

is it part of the human condition to crave to be more than
    you are?
do you know how it feels to want to be less?
most days, I teeter on the edge between wanting to take up
    more space and
wanting to take up none at all
which
makes me think it's a fine line.
either the neighbour's fence or
a seesaw,
or the edge of the bathtub
where I so often get stuck.

I can't decide whether I want to reach for the door handle or circle down the drain.

the sun,
a burning sphere of red and yellow,
fascinating
yet nobody can get close enough to touch.
she lights up half the day
but never rests.
her light bounces off rivers
and soaks into skin.
there are few places she cannot reach.
she is the heart of the entire galaxy,
without her we cease to exist.
the chemical energy she produces
is enough to illuminate seven billion faces.
she is burning and thriving,

I am trying to learn from her.

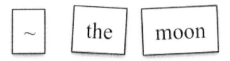

the moon
has many secrets.
I know this because I have seen her dark side.
we share intimate truths
as I hang out of my open window at 2am,
yearning for something bigger.
I tell her my troubles,
as she reminds me I am not the only sad soul who does
    this,
that from her surface to her core,
she holds the most vulnerable pieces of everybody.
this is supposed to be a comfort
and yet
I can't seem to shake the fact
I wish I had her all to myself.

my cousin passed when I was 10.
slipped between a place of here and
a place I didn't understand yet.
tearing a hole into a part of my brain
I didn't even know I could feel.
that day, you encouraged me to slide my Heelys on to my
    feet and
despite my puffy red eyes and throbbing head,
pushed me down the slope outside of your house.
you pulled me from a place I couldn't breathe in.
this was the same thing for us as an outstretched hand,
or a soft hug.

this is not about that.

unlike most friendships,
we grew into each other instead of growing apart.
11 years, 200 miles,
distance means nothing.
no time passes by us.
we can meet and grace through every long overdue subject
    in detail,
parting with the knowledge it will never be the last time.

handstands on bright days,
a handmade sled on cold ones.
a situational friendship by choice
and never forced,
except maybe
when we were 12
and had 4 nights left sleeping in the same tent.

you'd used my straw
and it was safe to say I was not happy about it.

dancing in the garden to footloose
will always be one of my purest forms of happiness.
bad karaoke, made up plays,
long nights of sharing pensive secrets and thoughtless
    laughter.
cooking without a recipe.
making transient art together,
filing it in places neither of us even remember anymore.
and I was always jealous of your bravery.
when climbing to the top of the tyre wall for our Scouts
    initiation was impossible for me,
you came to meet me at my level.
even so, I still looked up to you
and I did and still do make a mental note to thank you for
    your empathy.

memories hang like bunting
soon too heavy to hold up.
when that time comes,
we will repurpose the fabric,
sew it into something we can both wear.
embroider care instructions onto the label,
such as 'make a cup of tea first thing in the morning'
or 'order extra ketchup'.

caring for you is a feeling more than a set of instructions.
it is telling you the things I would like to hear,
understanding what you need before you even say it.
something ingrained deeply that doesn't require an ounce
    of thought or contemplation.

you are
an abstract painting in every colour,
hanging delicately in an open room
every place is more beautiful with you in it.

you are
the kind of person to say hi to a cat on the street
but will look first to make sure nobody is watching.
please know that you do not have to dim your exuberance
     for fear of judgement.

you are
a mirror most days.
comfort comes when I look into you and see myself,
feeling in explosions.
the purest intentions with the kindest heart,
I always feel heard with you,
always wanted.

nothing I say could ever elegantly reduce you to a poem,
accurately reflecting your being with words.
you possess something so much more than even art could
     show.
for now, I don't think I could say anything more profound
     than
thank you for bestowing your creativity and wonderful
     existence on this earth.
it is a better place for it.

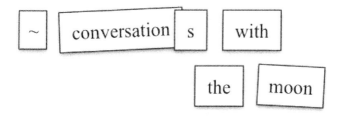

the moon is peeking through my curtains at 1:43am
while my mind is too infatuated to sleep.
she is asking me questions like;
"do you wonder how many times
he has looked at me and thought
I was beautiful?",
"do you wish you could see his face
lit up by my light?",
"do you want to know what he is like in the dark?".
I answer her yes, yes, yes
but she does not stop.
"do you think he has ever been in love?"
…
"probably with you," I say.

you can tell a lot about a person by their hands.
two separate masterpieces on the end of each wrist.
they have felt everything,
tiny hands wrapped around big thumbs,
sand slipping between small fingers
like time in an hourglass.
the way you use yours,
the way you unwrap a gift,
softly, slowly, savouringly,
yet rip off my clothes
as if there is hardly any time left.
your grip on my hips,
my neck, my hair,
I can feel your pulse through each palm, each fingertip.
it is as if your hands are my rib cage,
responsible for the blood pumping,
enclosed around my heart,
squeezing to aid the beating.

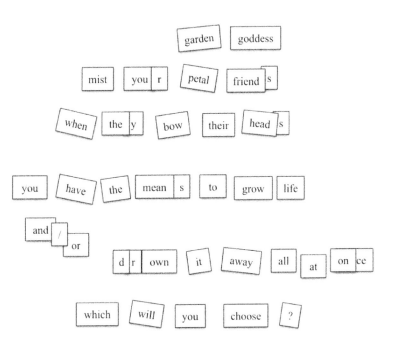

garden goddess

mist you r petal friend s

when the y bow their head s

you have the mean s to grow life

and / or d r own it away all at on ce

which will you choose ?

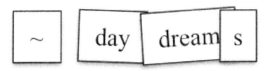

most of my daydreams
consist of you and I,
your soapy hand brushing mine
as you pass me another plate to dry.

in the tiny kitchen,
of our quaint one bed flat,
we clear up after dinner
in our own shared habitat.

I pass you the towel
to dry your hands,
you hang it over your shoulder
and we start tomorrow night's dinner plans.

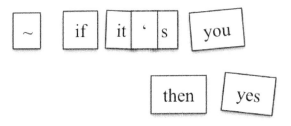

do you remember what it feels like
to jump without fear of falling?

I haven't had grazed knees since I was like, 7 probably,
but something about the childlike character that day
means there I was at 21,
pretending to glance at my watch
and
wait for a train that will never come.
on the old, abandoned train track,
we waited patiently until
something
made me pass my bag to you
and spontaneously leap between old train platforms,
only just making it
and landing sprawled on the gravel.
after grazing the skin off both my knees,
you asked if it hurt
and all I could say in between giggles was
"in a really good way".

maybe it was because
in the car an hour before,
you asked me shyly
if I would like to be your girlfriend,
an innocent, naive air around you.

or maybe because
when we got back to the car,

31

we kissed until the windows steamed.
just like the titanic,
painting me in French kisses,
a confident, knowing air around you.
a warmth pounding in my knees that replicated my heart
and maybe somewhere
else.
I jumped and fell into you
carelessly,
without a shred of thought or intention,
just pure feeling.
I have never fallen so fast,
reaching terminal velocity
blindly,
face first into chest,
broken ribs.
any faster and I would have broken my own heart.

I could say I love you more than life itself
but you make that a lie.
you make me love life
and from dark rabbit holes,
and thinking myself into graves,
that is an incredible feat.
I am not used to watching the blood trickle down my legs
like it has so many times before and
feeling so pure about it.
our love is like freshly baked bread,
constantly reinventing,
kneading new loaf after loaf,
hot from the oven,
dripping with melted butter.
two liquids poured in the same cup,
I want to merge into you,
maybe mould your hands out of wet clay,
just so I can touch them a while.

when you turned to me and asked
"want to, like… grow old together?"
I wanted to turn to you and tell you
that the skeleton of my vows are already folded neatly
on the corner of my desk.

if growing old means growing in,
drinking tea from yellow mugs on the porch,
or coaxing blue-eyed children to eat broccoli,
then yes.
if it's you, then yes.

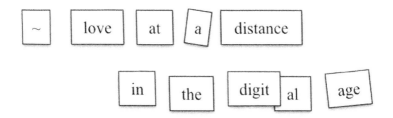

you fall asleep on the other side of my screen,
like you do most nights.
your eyes shut reluctantly
and your breathing starts to slow.
a smile creeps across your face
as you drift to a place
that I wish I could go with you.
I lay here thinking
if it feels like this
just to be able to see your sleepy smile
from 168 miles away,
it will be infinite happiness
when you get to weigh down the pillow next to mine
every single night.

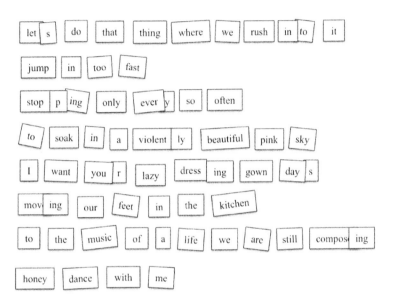

let s do that thing where we rush in to it

jump in too fast

stop p ing only ever y so often

to soak in a violent ly beautiful pink sky

I want you r lazy dress ing gown day s

mov ing our feet in the kitchen

to the music of a life we are still compos ing

honey dance with me

you are my toolbox.
saw away the broken parts,
sand down the edges.
glue me back together when I've fallen apart again,
level me back to my senses.

you already have everything you need
inside you
to fix me.

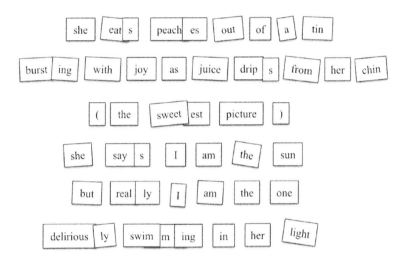

she eat s peach es out of a tin

burst ing with joy as juice drip s from her chin

(the sweet est picture)

she say s I am the sun

but real ly I am the one

delirious ly swim m ing in her light

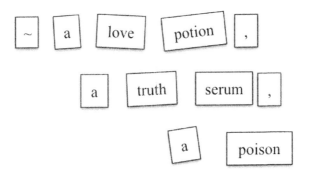

~ a love potion ,
a truth serum ,
a poison

our love was peach juice.
the sweetest, stickiest,
dripping from my middle finger,
sliding down your chin.

leaking over our pages, sticking together,
beautiful lines of rounded calligraphy now smudged and
    crisp at the edges.
when we tried to pull them apart, they ripped.

sometimes I can't even touch my own body because my
    hands feel too much like yours,
and I used to hold my own hand to soothe me back to
    sleep
but now it is my (your) hands that keep me awake.

a love like peach juice
is a sugar rush
until the
bruised,
sour,
inevitable,
crash.

we rush ed grace less *ly* through this love

delirious ly fast

passion ate ly accidental *in* ever y colour

gentle was not a harmony

our sweet heart s could play

so we slow ed and we stop p ed

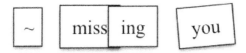

missing you is kinda like missing a dark night sky in June.
I wouldn't give up the peach sunset
or the dark silhouette of a lover against it
for a clean pitch-black slate.

you are less of a constant ache,
more of a swift and infrequent melancholic breeze
inviting the hairs on the back of my neck to dance
until I let my hair down,
shake out the last thoughts of you.

since missing you,
I recognise the passing of time
as less than linear
and more of fine powder,
rising, dusting,
coating everything we left on the shelf.
some days it is ash,
a harsh reminder of neglected memories,
but most days it is icing sugar,
sweet and delicate,
meets my tongue with contentment.

missing you might be forever,
but at least it is sweet.

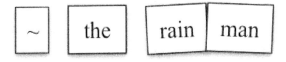

you forecast sun
but didn't prepare for the chance of rain.
when it rains,
you say I am the reason the heavens opened,
that I told the rain to fall.
it is my fault because I cannot stop it from falling
and I am simply just letting it drown me.
how can I control a force as great as nature?
you hand me a broken umbrella and wonder why I am still
   wet.

I am dripping,
my clothes are soaked down to my skin
and still, you pour a bucket of water over my head
as if you expect it to dry me.

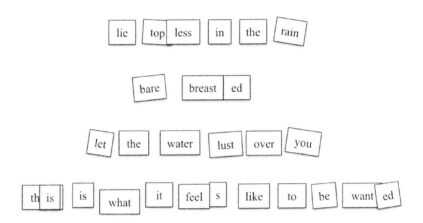

lie top less in the rain

bare breast ed

let the water lust over you

this is what it feel s like to be want ed

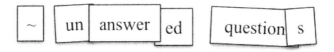

~ un answer ed question s

I want to forget you
but my mind constantly asks questions like
I wonder if those yellow flowers at your breakfast table
    reminded you of me
and I wonder if you couldn't look at them or you couldn't
    look away.
what are you thinking about in bed at night?
I wonder if you imagine me tucked my own bed
and whether you think about what I'm going to wear
    tomorrow
or whether I will wake early enough to drink my coffee at
    home.
I wonder if you walk slow down the street and hope you
    will bump into me,
even to see a glimpse of my face.
when you walk into a shop and one of my favourite songs
    plays above your head,
do you feel anything at all?
are you happy?
I wonder if when a pretty girl approaches you with hair
    like cinnamon and eyes the colour of a rainforest,
do you still wish you could see the sea instead?
when you turn your head in those first moments of
    consciousness each morning,
do you still expect to see me?
have you changed?
I wonder if you see a different future now,
a different baby, maybe with green eyes but still wild hair,
I wonder if your body is finally a calm beach,
swaying palm trees and slow salty waves
or is it still the raging tsunami I once knew.
I wish I could just ask you

but we both know things can never be the same,
so everything now resides as an unanswered question
thoughts remaining static in my head.

the memory of you is still hanging off me
like a tag I forgot to cut off.
lately I'm not even sure I want to.
nothing about us was predictable
and my mind changed like the weather did that Friday
but I look for you everywhere,
even in places I know you won't be.
I go to our beach sometimes,
plant my feet into the sand and wait.
I imagine you're probably in bed with another,
spending Sundays like we used to.
I don't blame you,
but I'll be here,
swaying patiently as a palm tree would,
waiting for the day you come and plant your feet next to
    mine
so we can grow together
instead of growing apart.

thoughts of you come and go,
even still.
just like you would cum
and then you would go
smoke your cigarette,
leave me dripping.
full and empty at the same time,
nothing more than a scrunched-up tissue
that you'd use to clean yourself up.
except tissues don't bruise
when you touch them the way you touched me.

you treated me like property
you were breaking in to,
setting the curtains alight and
leaving a trail of smoke in your wake.
that was not what I wanted
and yet I couldn't say it
for fear you would like it
when I said no.
breath of fire,
no amount of cold showers
could cool the burns
and stop the heat rash spreading.

the only way I could remain in control
was by not saying anything at all,
was by giving you the key
so you wouldn't break down the door,
was pretending I wanted it
so you would not have all the power.

since then,
I've installed a house alarm
and heavy-duty locks.

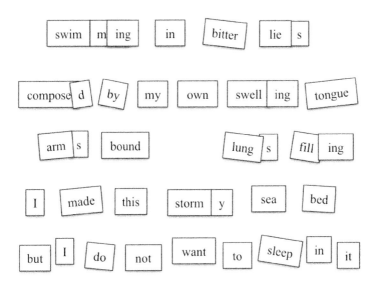

swim m ing in bitter lie s

compose d by my own swell ing tongue

arm s bound lung s fill ing

I made this storm y sea bed

but I do not want to sleep in it

jealousy is acid
both
burning through metal
and
causing intrepid hallucinations
of every bold-faced thing
you've ever had the nerve to imagine,
humiliating you into nothing.

to day is like
boil ing hot water on skin
red raw
scream s that rip through the blood smear ed sky
ache ing all over
trudg ing through time
with the urge to crush the sun
just for shine ing

duck egg blue is less of a colour to me and more of a feeling. it is calm mixed with the softness of baby skin. kitchen in morning light, coffee on cold days. duck egg blue is spring and autumn, tepid water, an in-between. the sound of birds migrating in an arrow formation, falling back and re-joining. breaking out of shells. soft colour wrapped around a hard exterior. baby bird breaking out. of. it's. shell. something small can still be so powerful. I am in a shell, duck egg blue. am I strong enough? not sure how to break out of this one.

sad should not be a language I am fluent in

a song I still know all the word s to

eve n after all this time

I listen and make note s like

one day I will need to accompany death

on his last ever jo b

like I will need to perform for him a master piece

sing his loud horn et s nest sound

scream in to the ears of each grave

I do not want to hear it any more

please be quiet let me rest

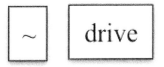

one day you're driving in your car
screaming at the moon
because you can't believe you're alive
with the privilege to soak in the light reflected from her
    surface.

and the next,
the weight of her looking at you is too heavy to bear,
the embarrassment is hot on your cheeks
and it makes you want to take a left turn
where there isn't one.

daisy chains

I have been anchoring weightless feeling s down

with a broken cord

not familiar with such buoyancy

pumped full of helium rising

white knuckles holding on to an invisible string

blue face holding on to used air

when I have intrusive thoughts, I look to the shadows of
things.
the way the light bounces off objects onto others,
decide what shades I would use and what combination of
    pigment I would mix
to make that specific hue.

instead of
jump from this balcony,
crash your car,
it is
one part ultramarine blue mixed with one part titanium
    white,
some cadmium red for a purple.
it is
fan brush, filbert, palette knife,
find the shadows of things until it is quiet.

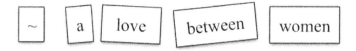

I realised I was gay
at the National Gallery in London,
stood in front of 'Susanna at her Bath'
by Francesco Hayez,
I stared until I felt warm in places.

I turned to my boyfriend,
told him softly I was questioning my sexuality
and he broke up with me
right in front of Susanna.
eyes burning on us, this is when I first became
    entertainment.
she was the only one looking who understood,
this is when I only became worth something if eyes were
    on me.

when I told my male friend
I fell in love with a girl
with a smile of angels and
eyes like home,
that she reminded me of Susanna,
his face lit up
and the 'can I watch?' came out of his mouth like instant
    ejaculation.
I instantly turned into a spectacle, an object
if i wasn't one already.
I should have left
but I laughed and shrugged, because I didn't know how to
    fight yet.

have you ever known the pain
of a lover dropping your hand in public
because it's safer to pretend you're just friends
when a group of grown men walk past
who don't know how to mind their own business?

and when they catch you
fingers interlaced, thumb rubbing gently against back of
    hand,
they jeer and gesture,
placing themselves in situations they were not invited to,
making places feel warm then hot then angry.
when they catch you they will hurt you.
being hurt by love should be left to those in love,
not those outside of it.
especially not by those who think
dykes are made for men's pleasure,
purely to play with.
that we do not exist outside of pornhub,
long blonde hair, sharp acrylic nails,
this is not what a love between women looks like.

a love between women is powerful.
it is bright red flames, hot pink silk.
if you mess with it you will get burned.
we are not made for your consumption,
not fruits that you can devour and throw out of your car
    window
to rot in the shrubs.
we are the shrubs.
growing, winding, intertwining,
we are not made for your entertainment.
you will leave us alone.

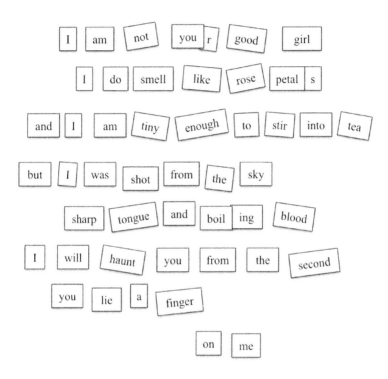

I am not you r good girl
I do smell like rose petal s
and I am tiny enough to stir into tea
but I was shot from the sky
sharp tongue and boil ing blood
I will haunt you from the second
you lie a finger
on me

when the sad daffodils bow their heads in mourning,
you know bad things are happening in the world.
I want to tap the tip of their chins
and lift back to the sky
but the sun isn't making enough light for any of us.
so my head droops, chin to chest
and all I can do is wait for some magic.

I wash my hands more frequently than those rich white
    men shift blame.
the cracks that form in my skin resemble mosaic ice plates,
melting,
drifting,
at least six feet apart
or six feet under.
it's a simple enough choice for most.

when 'I can't breathe' is a valid argument to not wear a
    mask,
but not good enough when a man sworn to protect is
    kneeling on your neck,
what protects us then?

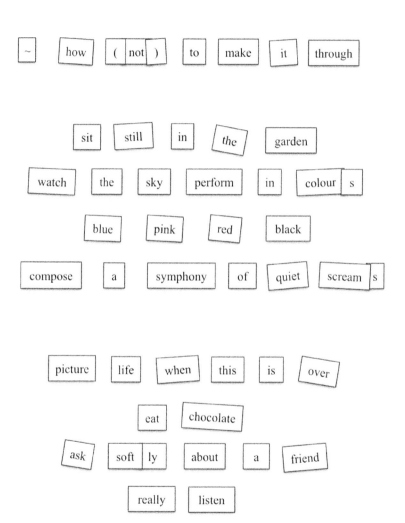

~ how (not) to make it through

sit still in the garden
watch the sky perform in colour s
blue pink red black
compose a symphony of quiet scream s

picture life when this is over
eat chocolate
ask soft ly about a friend
really listen

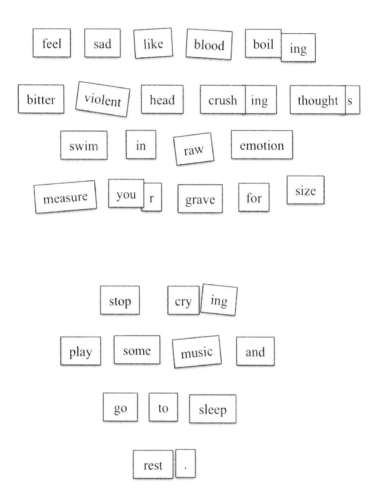

feel sad like blood boil ing

bitter violent head crush ing thought s

swim in raw emotion

measure you r grave for size

stop cry ing

play some music and

go to sleep

rest .

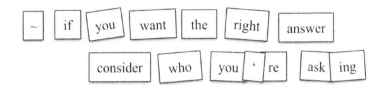

I asked the moon
if I could see my loved ones soon,
she said "I don't know,
I can barely see anyone from up here."

I asked the sky
if it was okay to cry,
she said "I don't know,
they don't seem to like when I rain."

I asked the rain
if it felt any kind of blame
it said, "I don't know,
we are too busy to care."

I asked the sun
if it was okay to run,
she said "I don't know,
they don't seem to like when I hide."

it occurred to me
that it could be a possibility
I was asking the wrong questions
to the wrong entities.

daisy chains

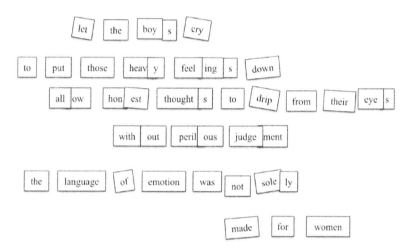

let the boy s cry
to put those heav y feel ing s down
all ow hon est thought s to drip from their eye s
with out peril ous judge ment
the language of emotion was not sole ly
made for women

I am a white woman.
I was not born with a silver spoon in my mouth
but I was born with white skin
and that's sort of the same thing.
this is not supposed to be about me
but it always is anyway
and that's the problem.

we cannot stay warm and cosy
in our white linen bed sheets
when black people are continuously denied entry,
healthcare
or air,
basic fucking human rights.

the colours I see you in
are not synonymous with your pigment,
but your personality.
an inviting red warmth,
or a cool easy blue air around you,
soft pink purple glow, radiating love,
yellow beaming smiling light.
these are the colours you can control,
not a pigment you were born with.

I will not make this about me.
complacency in this situation is not enough
and I will be a fist in the air,
a pillar of solidarity.
I cannot become an eraser to remove all that history,

but I can smudge the harsh lines of segregation between
    us.

we are not black or white
but black and white mixed with every other shade of the
    rainbow.
we can bleed into each other.
we can merge together.
I will always stand up for you.
I will always let you sit down.

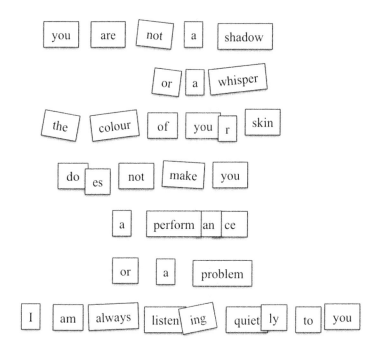

you are not a shadow
or a whisper
the colour of your skin
does not make you
a performance
or a problem
I am always listening quietly to you

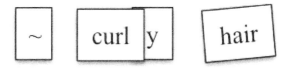

curly hair
twisting and winding like the branches of a tree,
reaching upwards and outwards trying to touch the sun.
a hundred thousand individual strands
each coiled in a different direction.

my hands quickly found a home there.
tiny ringlets looped around fingers like vines,
tracing the soft edges of each helix,
bouncing springs spiralled in no particular orientation.

the next time you think about taming the garden growing
    on your head,
remember those roots are dug into you
because nature trusts you are the perfect environment
to help those trees flourish and thrive.

daisy chains

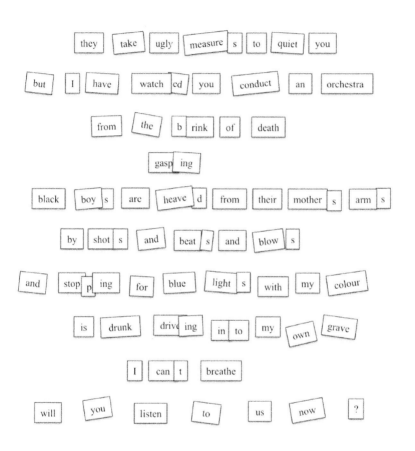

they take ugly measure s to quiet you

but I have watch ed you conduct an orchestra

from the b rink of death

gasp ing

black boy s are heave d from their mother s arm s

by shot s and beat s and blow s

and stop p ing for blue light s with my colour

is drunk driv ing in to my own grave

I can t breathe

will you listen to us now ?

~ after George Floyd and all of those victim to police
brutality

the new year is just
a glorified Monday.
a holiday once again romanticised to sell you back to
    yourself
but you are still you.
no amount of crash dieting or reduced skin care products
can fix the fundamental problem of unrealistic societal
    norms.
they want to see us consume to no end,
as satisfaction is a revolution
in the eyes of capitalism.
you are not obliged to comply.

after the last harrowing year,
we should be making an attempt to focus on appreciation
and contentment for the things we already have.
is it such a rebellion
to wish to stay exactly as you are?

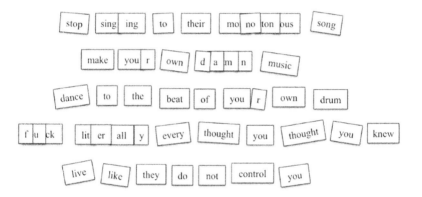

stop singing to their monotonous song
make your own damn music
dance to the beat of your own drum
fuck literally every thought you thought you knew
live like they do not control you

I opened a new book, dog eared the first page and put it back on the shelf. spring flew like the baby bird from it's nest. August is an illusion of candles and birthday cake and temporary happiness. I will pretend this is what life is supposed to feel like until I am proven otherwise. my cat is sixteen angels stacked on top of one another in a fur coat. twenty-two is just the outer ring of the tree trunk, cut into me and I am still full of myself. cut into me and I am made of birthday cake. I fear I'm losing grip of reality.

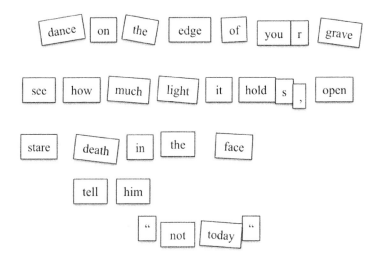

dance on the edge of you r grave

see how much light it hold s , open

stare death in the face

tell him

" not today "

they say that you don't know what you have until it's gone
   which
always makes me look at the things I love a little
   differently.
like I know it will someday be gone,
like I should try to hold myself a little looser.
I don't think that's the point of that phrase but I think it
   nonetheless.

they say that you don't know what you have until it's gone
   but
sometimes I think the opposite is true.
how you can become so infatuated with the idea of
something that you think you know what you have but
when it's gone you realise you never really knew it at all.
like treading water until your legs are sore but realising
you could touch the bottom the whole time.

at the end of the day,
after everything else is stripped away,
we only ever really truly have the present moment.
why does it always feel parallel to my body?
why does it take so much to see it for so little?
why does it always feel like I can't really touch it?
the unreachable enigma that is the art of being present.

I want to look back and say I've lived but
I'm always holding on too tight or trying to let go.

how bittersweet to miss a moment whilst you're still living
it.
how bittersweet to realise you've never really lived it at
all.

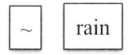

for the daughter I am yet to conceive -

rain
sweet thoughts
onto the tiny seeds you will plant.
build a forest with what I will teach you,
teach the world how to climb a tree.

you will be a force to be reckoned with.
both feet planted firmly but head in the clouds.
you will see the impermanence of them, just like the sky
    does,
just like time.
time is a privilege
and privilege is not something that you will always have
but you will see the permanence of your impact,
loud, fierce, powerful
like thunder rolling,
raining to water the seeds you will sow.

rain
I will shower you with love
like the sun's light.
watch your flowers bloom and
grow out of my white picket fence garden.
take the world from my hands.

not yet a mother

but I still dream soft sounds.

that first gentle cry like music,

tiny fingers make a fist,

running water with honey

to lather pink skin,

putting a sweet smelling head to rest,

heating milk at one am.

these are the ways I will love you.

for now,

I wake and I ache

in a quiet room.

you can hate it, change it, destroy it
but this body is not yours anyway.
it is connected to the earth,
like gravity is keeping an eye on it.
a gift given as a vessel for your mind,
entrusted to you
in the hope you will do good things with it.
until the earth reclaims it,
reducing it back to dirt and soil and water,
back to where it came from.

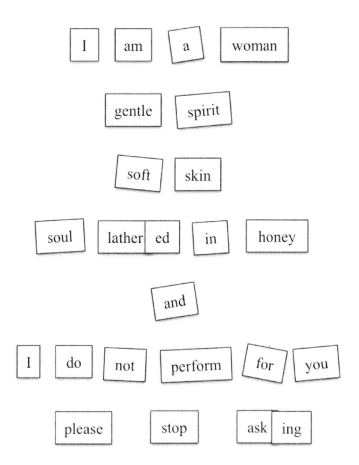

I am a woman

gentle spirit

soft skin

soul lather ed in honey

and

I do not perform for you

please stop ask ing

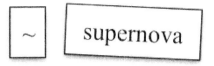

imagine
floating among the stars,
quiet,
except
every time you reach your fingers out to touch
they jingle like bells,
sweet melodies
that nobody else will ever hear.

in reality
this infinite universe is hot and fiery,
harsh and unforgiving.
even the stupendous size of our galaxy
is unfathomable.
although it looks sweet and milky
like you could stir it into your tea,
it won't hesitate to suffocate you
if you go too deep.

the sheer vastness of the universe
might make you feel insignificant.
but the truth is,
matter cannot be created or destroyed.
when a star dies,
explodes into miles and miles of debris,
a supernova,
the dramatic and catastrophic destruction
marked by one final titanic eruption,
the formation of heavy elements and energy transfer
are used to make us.
so it can be soft.
the stars give back life.

we are all made of stardust
and a little bit of fire.

baby,
why do you keep telling me you feel lonely?
how can you feel lonely
when you have a destruction of wildcats
underneath your skin
that purr heavily when you take care of yourself?
you
have a colony of fireflies in your eyes
that light up your face when you laugh.
there is a flock of songbirds that perch on you voice box,
you just have to let them sing.
embrace the school of fish in your stomach,
they are swishing their fins
in rhythm with your heartbeat.
I know sometimes you have grizzly bears in your throat,
soothe them with a song and a little bit of honey.
baby, I promise,
there's no need to feel lonely
when you are home to so many other communities.

~ | poetry

you can call whatever you want poetry,
I guess.
your plagiarised three-word quote,
the entire thesaurus, cover to cover,
your first-born child.
don't expect to pass it a torch,
for it to make an impact.
don't expect it to change the world.

find it inside you
to write about the things that feel like
fire under skin,
bright light in eyes,
the stagnant water you've waded through.
use your words to process,
slow down,
gather your thoughts that seem
scattered
like wildflowers over a meadow.

if you don't think you're the best writer to ever exist
then you're doing something wrong.
write in colours that
nobody else has ever seen.
write loud.
make them listen.
use your voice or step back,
let someone else use theirs.

thoughts are like clouds.
some are pure,
white and fluffy,
radiating with light from the sun.

others are angry,
dark and menacing,
you wait for the thunder.

occasionally there is nothing but a clear blue sky,
and these are the calm days.

the thing about clouds
is that they all turn to rain,
a downfall of heavy letters
waiting to be recycled
into another passing thought.

has anyone ever asked you
to describe yourself in three words?
asked you to reduce your existence
to fit on the back of a playing card
that they can put back into the break of a deck
and shuffle out of their memory?

I refuse. you want me to define myself?

I am memorable / unpredictable / a beautiful contradiction
/ a perfect tragedy.

an entire art gallery / every brushstroke / every feeling /
every frame.
similarly, I contain multitudes / very expensive forgeries /
prying thieves / and overpriced coffee.

constantly contemplating / always waiting / missed trains /
daisy chains,
an unmade bed.

always tired / definitely on the brink of getting fired / a
panic attack at 7am.

I am a survivor / the sun that rises each morning despite
the moon coming back to bed / a ~~worrier~~ warrior / aspiring
to be the human equivalent of the smell of spring.

try fitting me on the back of that playing card with all of
this sunshine in my back pocket.
try fitting me anywhere at all.

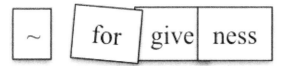

I think I'm finally at an age
where I can forgive my younger self.
this is a sweet relief from lying awake at night
anxious about that one joke I made that one time in high
    school that nobody laughed at.

I can forgive her for the slit-like scars
she left on my thighs,
making us fail that exam
because she took too many of her meds at once,
for missing half our classes because her cuts were bleeding
    through her school tights
or she was too busy having a panic attack in the toilets.

I still feel things the way she did,
pins and needles,
rain in my body,
water falling on an empty stomach
but I know how to carry them now.
I can pick up a pen
instead of a pencil sharpener or a pair of scissors
and I know when to let go of them.

sometimes I worry that I haven't changed at all
like I could still rip my body apart from the inside
but then I catch myself laughing to myself in the shower
and I watch my laughter circle the drain
instead of the blood there used to be
and I realise it is the sweetest song.
I wish I could play it on repeat for her
like she used to play Hannah Montana on her pink CD
    player

but
I don't want to tell her what I know now.
I want her to choke and almost drown and learn how to
    swim
because I'm still scared of the ocean
but I have swam lengths across this stormy sea
and I wouldn't change it for anything.

note to my younger self: I forgive you. you do make it
through, and my god, it is so sweet.

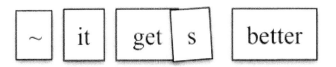

I have spent years
trying to convince myself I am allowed to take up space in
    this world.
before,
I would suck in my stomach
and carve out the fat in my thighs,
tell my mother I am full
when I have not eaten for days.
what I really mean is
I am full of hatred,
full of sadness.
I would tell my mother I am sick
when I really meant
I am sick of myself,
sick of telling myself to shrink shrink shrink
when all I could do was grow.
when I did eat
I would watch it come back up
and feel empty in all the wrong places.

now,
I do not treat calories as currency
like I am on a budget.
I do not have to lie to my mother.
my stomach,
my heart,
my soul,
are full
and yet I feel so much lighter.

now,
I can allow myself to grow.
I take up so much space.

I can encourage my thoughts to stretch out and up,
I want them to be noticed.
I want to be listened to.

I promise you, even though you don't want to hear it,
it does get so much better.

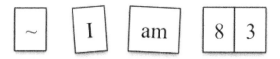

I am 83.
the house has not looked like a mess for six weeks,
since the last time the grandkids came to visit
and left trails of Lego and messy fingerprints up the walls.

I potter in the garden,
making sure my hydrangeas are nothing less than perfectly
    even
and every weed has been pulled.
I watch my cat pounce at a butterfly
and marvel at her innocence.

I smile at the young newlywed couple over the fence
and remember each of my loves in turn,
letting the sweet memories ooze into me
like peach juice in my mouth
just for a few minutes.

I go to turn on the oven
for a dinner that only I will eat
and as I pass by the hallway mirror I see a weathered
    version of myself
wrinkles and dark circles and lines
but I do not see them as this.
I recognise love lines, life lines,
stretch marks given to me by lives that I made,
lives that have flown to other places.

I do not remember why I cried so much when I was 21.
why I gave myself scars and bruises,
wished I was dead.
but as my heart swells with beautiful memories of my life,
I forgive myself for this.

my world is much smaller now
and I may be more alone than I was back then
but I am definitely not more lonely.

daisy chains

Kay is a 22-year-old writer from the UK. She started posting magnetic poetry on her Instagram account in 2018 but has been writing since her early teens. She is a novice painter, as can be seen on the cover.

From an early age Kay has used poetry as her own personal therapy, to process her thoughts and often turn life's darker moments into art. The book reflects a journey from a girl to a young woman, as she faces the trials and tribulations of growing up in today's world, with many self-discoveries made along the way.

She currently lives in a small house full of flowers, art, magnetic poetry and her cat, Tink.

This book was a decade in the making. It's her first step into the world of publishing, with many more exciting works to come…

You can find her online on Instagram – @daisychainkay